DEATH VALLEY
NATIONAL PARK

An Interpretive History

BY
JAMES W. CORNETT

Opposite: Desert holly, a pale blue-gray shrub widespread throughout
Death Valley, and hardy saltbrush grow in a cinder field near Ubehebe Crater.
Above: Cracked mud forms patterns in a depression in the Death Valley Sand Dunes.

PHOTOGRAPHY CREDITS

Above: The remains of a mesquite tree at sunset.

Left: A beetle crosses a sand dune, leaving a distinctive trail.
Opposite: A one-way road leads into Twenty Mule Team Canyon.

© 1996 Death Valley Natural History Association
All Rights Reserved.
No part of this publication may be reproduced in any form without permission from the publisher.

Project Coordinator: Esy Fields

Produced for the Death Valley
Natural History Association
by Companion Press
Santa Barbara, California

Publisher/Editor Jane Freeburg
Designed by Lucy Brown

Printed and bound in Hong Kong through Bolton Associates, San Rafael, California

ISBN 1-878900-33-1

96 97 98 99 00   •   5 4 3 2 1

CONTENTS

Death Valley National Park was established for "...the preservation of the unusual features of scenic, scientific, and educational interest therein" and "...the proper care, management, and protection of unusual features of scientific interest." Under the National Park Service's Organic Act, the Service is charged with providing for the public use and enjoyment—and resource preservation—of the area.

To provide for the public use and enjoyment of the area while preserving its resources is not an easy task. All of the responsibility for preserving this area does not lie with only the National Park Service. In fact, a majority of this responsibility lies with you, its user. Please respect the amazing resources that are made available to you by not altering them in any way.

The best way to remember your trip through Death Valley is either through your own photographs or through the photographs and text in a book such as this one. Enjoy Death Valley, truly a land of extremes.

Sincerely,

Richard H. Martin, Superintendent
Death Valley National Park

*To drop into Death Valley...on a summer
afternoon is almost like entering a furnace.*

Edmund C. Jaeger, *The North American Deserts*, 1957

Death Valley is a land of contrasts and extremes. Consider temperature. In the center of Death Valley lies the tiny community of Furnace Creek, where on July 10, 1913 the official air temperature climbed to 134 degrees Fahrenheit. This was, and still is, the hottest temperature ever recorded in North America and, at that time, anywhere on earth.

Then consider rainfall, or the lack thereof. It will be obvious to any visitor that Death Valley is dry—with its clear blue skies, sparse vegetation, and rocky streambeds. Rainfall on the valley floor might not exceed two inches for an entire year, with a long-term annual average of just 1.84 inches. Such meager precipitation earns Death Valley its ominous reputation as one of the driest spots on the continent.

Elevations, too, are extreme. Just a few miles south of Furnace Creek lies Badwater, the lowest spot in the western hemisphere. At this site the elevation plummets 282 feet below sea level and the ground is white with salt. Yet just a few miles to the west stands Telescope Peak with a summit reaching 11,049 feet, an alpine environment of snow and frost where rugged bristlecone pines cling to rocky slopes. These two points give Death Valley National Park the distinction of containing a mountain peak that rises higher and steeper than any other peak in a national park in the contiguous forty-eight states.

A rising and falling ribbon of highway characterizes

a drive across Death Valley, and is the best way to illustrate the Park's elevational extremes. Just outside the park in the Owens Valley the elevation is 3,600 feet. Stretching east, State Highway 180 climbs to nearly 6,000 feet as it crosses the park boundary in the Argus Mountains. Then suddenly it plummets 4,000 feet into the Panamint Valley only to—just as suddenly—rise up in the adjoining Panamint Mountains. The highway climbs over 3,000 feet in only six linear miles before reaching Towne Pass at nearly 5,000 feet. Facing east, the drop to the floor of Death Valley itself falls more than 5,000 feet—to below sea level. To the east of Death Valley the Amargosa Range rises more than 4,000 feet. Leaving park boundaries, the road descends another 2,000 feet into Nevada and the Amargosa Valley. This roller coaster ride reflects the extreme topography of Death Valley National Park, and offers a driving experience unlike any other in America.

No other place in America can boast of such extremes, and few places can match Death Valley's own strange beauty. The lush green vegetation that dominates so many other landscapes is absent here. Yet in its place Death Valley displays the magical yellows, oranges, and browns of the earth—all presented in brilliant contrast to startling blue skies. In some areas of the park the rawness of the eroded earth suggests a time before human life began; a time that seems closer to the creation of the earth. Indeed, Death Valley is a land like no other.

Opposite: The view north from Golden Canyon.
Above: Winter sunrise at the dunes. Top: Sand patterns.

*...it is a land of ever-changing colors
from sunrise to sunset.*

Charles B. Hunt, *Death Valley: Geology, Ecology,
Archaeology,* 1975

Although visitors may expect to find vast regions of low, hot, desert terrain here, Death Valley National Park offers much more. Incorporated within the Park are lofty mountains such as Telescope, Wildrose, and Grapevine Peaks, all of which rise over 8,000 feet above the valley floor. Lower temperatures and higher precipitation in the mountain environments support distinctly different plant species, from pinyon pine, juniper, and grizzly bear cactus at intermediate elevations to limber and ancient bristlecone pines on the mountaintops.

Geologists describe Death Valley's stark landscape as an "open textbook" of the forces that shape the earth's surface. Rocks and formations that are obscured by vegetation or obliterated by heavy rainfall in less arid regions are here laid bare. Fault scarps, volcanoes, and contorted rocks are easily viewed and, with a little help, easily understood.

Death Valley, unlike many other valleys, was not carved by a river, but formed as the result of fractures or "faults" in the Earth's brittle crust. Geologists term this kind of valley a fault basin or "graben." In the Death Valley region, movements along faults allowed one portion of the Earth's crust to slip or "down drop" past another. As portions or "blocks" of the crust were down-dropping to create valleys, they were also being tilted or "rotated" to the east. As the eastern edges of the crustal blocks tilted down, the western edges rose up—creating mountains. The Panamint Range

along the western edge of Death Valley National Park and the Amargosa Range along its eastern edge show the visible results of this process. Although much of the landscape of eastern California and Nevada is composed of this "basin and range" topography, Death Valley is the most dramatic example of the phenomenon.

Death Valley is young in terms of geologic time. The rounding and leveling forces of erosion, at work for a relatively short time here, have left Death Valley's rugged, precipitous landscape intact. Consider that our planet is approximately four and one-half billion years old, yet Death Valley was formed in just the last three million years, scarcely a grain of sand in the hourglass of earth history. Yet the rock itself may be much older than the valley. The rock layers that constitute the somber grey horizontal bands in the Black Mountains, visible from the paved road south of Badwater into Jubilee Pass, date back to the Precambrian period and are around 1.8 billion years old—six hundred times older than the valley itself. Although the initial uplifting of the mountains surrounding Death Valley began some eight to ten million years ago, it is only in the last three million years that they have risen in elevation so dramatically. Their relative youth—and the scarcity of precipitation which might otherwise smooth off their sharp edges—bring a stark and rugged beauty to these mountain slopes.

Opposite: Clouds move over the Last Chance Range and cottontop cactus. Above: Bands of colorful rock in the Panamint Mountains. Top: Rock colors at Artists Palette.

Above: Gnarled ancient bristlecone pines cling to the sub-alpine slopes high on Telescope Peak. Top: Salt creates intricate patterns on the cracked mud floor of Death Valley, the driest place in North America.

CREATION OF A DESERT

The mountains to the west of Death Valley are responsible for the arid conditions that prevail on the valley floor. Each storm traveling east off the Pacific Ocean must rise as it passes over the ranges in its path. As a storm climbs to higher altitudes, its air mass cools and its capacity to hold moisture decreases, resulting in the condensation of water into droplets. Most of these droplets fall as rain or snow when the storm ascends the western or "windward" slopes of the ranges. By the time the storm clouds reach the valley floor they have been wrung dry of their moisture. Meteorologists call this a "rain shadow" effect.

Storms traveling east off the Pacific Ocean encounter not just one but a series of mountain barriers before reaching Death Valley. The Coastal Ranges are the first obstacle, followed by the much higher Sierra Nevada Range. The Argus and Inyo Mountains are next in line with the Panamint Mountains standing as the last range over which a storm must pass before reaching Death Valley. In all, four rain shadow systems confront eastward-traveling storms. No wonder Death Valley is the driest place in North America, averaging less than two inches of precipitation per year!

SURROUNDING MOUNTAINS

Numerous peaks within Death Valley National Park reach sufficient altitude to support decidedly undesert-like vegetation. Telescope Peak in the Panamint Range, the highest point within Death Valley National Park, reaches 11,049 feet above sea level. Its upper slopes are clad with stands of bristlecone pine, a species of tree that occasionally exceeds 4,000 years of age, placing it among the oldest living things on our planet. Pinyon and limber pines, as well as juniper, can also be found throughout the high country of the Panamint Range. The Cottonwood

Mountains lie just to the north of the Panamints—their highest point, Tin Mountain, reaches 8,953 feet in elevation.

The mountains forming the eastern wall of Death Valley are not as tall as the Panamints, though they are certainly as steep. The Grapevine, Funeral, and Black Mountains, running north and south, are known collectively as the Amargosa Range. Grapevine Peak, near Scottys Castle, is the highest point in Death Valley's eastern mountains; it reaches an elevation of 8,738 feet, its slopes dotted with rugged limber pines. The Amargosa Range provides some of the most spectacular and accessible views of the valley floor below.

ALLUVIAL FANS

Death Valley is one of the best places in North America to observe alluvial fans. During unusually heavy storms, rain washes rocks, sand and gravel (alluvium) off mountainsides and down into can-yons. Where a canyon opens onto the valley floor the water spreads out, losing velocity and depositing the water-carried material at the canyon mouth. From a distance, these sloping deposits appear fan-shaped, hence the name alluvial fan. Although they may be obscured in other environments, the lack of vegetation in Death Valley makes these deposits readily observable here. Watch for alluvial fans at the mouths of east-facing canyons along the base of the Panamint Range to the west of Death Valley. A second spectacular group of fans rises from the salt pan to canyons in the Funeral Range along the east side of the valley.

DANTES VIEW

A dramatic vista within Death Valley National Park is found at Dantes View, situated almost 6,000 feet above the valley floor on the edge of the Black Mountains. The perspective is grand in the extreme, with a breathtaking view. Gazing to the

Saltbushes (foreground) and creosote bushes (mid-ground) rise up to meet the bajada at the base of 8,995-foot Tin Mountain. A bajada is formed when the alluvial fans emanating from several canyons coalesce to form a single broad plain. The plain at Tin Mountain's base is bisected by several dry washes.

Above: The vista from Dantes View, looking northwest over Death Valley toward the Panamint Range. Opposite, top: A shallow, salty pool at Badwater, 282 feet below sea level and the lowest point in the Western Hemisphere. Opposite, below right: Pickleweed grows along the edge of pools at Badwater.

west, one can view the winter snow on the Panamint Range and easily pick out Telescope Peak rising majestically over the barren salt flats of the valley floor. Below, strange patterns reveal a fascinating array of salt deposits including gypsum and rock salt that cover more than 200 square miles. Badwater lies straight down the mountainside. Large, black ravens often frequent the area rafting on the warm updrafts from the valley below. Officials of the Pacific Coast Borax Company named the viewpoint; they were said to have been inspired by the description of purgatory in Dante's *Inferno*.

BADWATER

The lowest point in the Western Hemisphere lies at Badwater in Death Valley National Park. At 282 feet below

sea level, this spot is testimony to the downward sliding of the valley floor along faults in the Earth's crust. Relatively speaking, the surface here has been dropping faster than sand, silt, and gravel washed out from canyon mouths can pile up. The small spring-fed pool at Badwater is the only remnant of an ancient lake that covered the floor of Death Valley at intervals during the Pleistocene Ice Age. Called "Lake Manly" by geologists, this body of water at one time reached nearly 100 miles in length and six to eleven miles in width with an estimated depth of nearly 600 feet. Abundant precipitation and cooler temperatures during the last ice age resulted in tremendous runoff not only in the surrounding mountains but in the Sierra Nevada mountains fifty miles west of Death Valley. Ancient rivers drain-

ing the eastern slopes of the Sierras had no outlet to the ocean, and flowed inland to the lowest point in the region—Death Valley. With the end of the last ice age and the spread of aridity in southwestern North America over the past ten thousand years, runoff decreased drastically. Coupled with soaring evaporation rates due to higher temperatures, this resulted in the drying up of ancient "Lake Manly" and the creation of a huge salt "playa" in its place.

Even though the pool at Badwater is exceedingly salty, plant and animal life are not absent. Wiggling soldier fly larvae abound and bronze water beetles can be seen searching for algae. Patches of ditch grass grow in clumps near the shore and the salt-tolerant pickleweed is found at the water's edge.

DEVILS GOLF COURSE

Devils Golf Course represents one of the most rugged textures on the surface of our planet. The jagged pinnacles are rock-hard salt crystals composed mostly of table salt (sodium chloride) with some silt mixed in. The salt layer is about three feet thick and rests on a bed of mud which underlies much of the valley. The salt pinnacles were originally formed by capillary action when a shallow lake disappeared due to increasing aridity about two thousand years ago. As the water evaporates, salt precipitates out as crystals, many of them forming sharp ridges and peaks. Occasional rains keep the crystals sharp. Some salt pinnacles reach nearly two feet in height and can easily cut through leather.

ZABRISKIE POINT

One of the most colorful and dramatic vistas in Death Valley National Park greets visitors at Zabriskie Point. Yellow

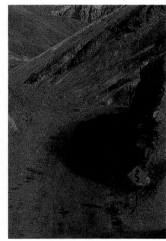

mud hills, uplifted within the last few million years, are part of the ancient lakebed sediments of the Pliocene Age Furnace Creek Formation that predate Ice Age "Lake Manly." The fine-grained muds and siltstone that comprise the hills prevent the absorption of much water; most runs off. Such surface run-off results in deep furrowing of the landscape, creating badlands that support almost no vegetation. To the west can be seen the salt beds on the valley floor and the towering Panamint Mountains. The point is named for the late Christian Brevoort Zabriskie, a onetime vice-president and general manager of the Pacific Coast Borax operations in Death Valley.

ARTISTS PALETTE

A few miles south of the Visitor Center lies the turnoff for Artists Drive, a paved, nine-mile driving excursion through one of the most colorful parts of Death Valley National Park. The road runs over steep alluvial fans, passes through washes, and winds down canyons bounded by mudhills. It climbs steadily above the valley floor, offering a sweeping view back across the salt flats. Multi-colored hills, representing 5,000-foot thick deposits of cemented gravels, ancient lake sediments, and volcanic debris here form the front of the Black Mountains. The rocks of the Artists Drive Formation have yielded diatoms and microscopic plants indicative of an environment which existed some ten to thirty million years ago. The exact composition of the multi-colored rock pigments at Artists Drive is still being researched. However, iron oxides are thought to be responsible for the reds, yellows, browns, blacks, and other intermediate shades. Purple hues are produced by magnesium. At other localities copper is often responsible for the green color of rocks but some geologists believe the greens of the Artist Drive Formation are the result of the breakdown of mica.

Opposite, top: Eroded mudstone forms undulating hills below Zabriskie Point, with a view of majestic Manly Beacon (right) and 11,049-foot Telescope Peak (upper left). Opposite, lower left: Formidable salt deposits on the valley floor at Devils Golf Course. Above, left: Minerals in the rock create the unusual color at Artists Palette. Above, right: Artists Drive winds among colorful mud hills at the base of the Black Mountains.

Right: As a storm gathers, sunset illuminates softly eroded mudstone hills below Zabriskie Point.

Below: The narrow entrance to Golden Canyon.

Opposite: Death Valley National Park's landscapes range from valleys to mountains. Spring snow west of the Eureka Valley covers a forest of Joshua Trees.

GOLDEN CANYON

Reflected afternoon light clearly justifies this canyon's name. The yellow mudstones and siltstones take on a golden hue at this time; in fact they almost glow. Like the eroded terrain at Zabriskie Point, Golden Canyon has been uplifted and carved within the last few million years. Prior to uplifting and long before creation of Lake Manly, sediments (including the forerunners of evaporite minerals such as borax and gypsum) were deposited in horizontal layers in ancient shallow lakes. Only after these beds were formed did uplift and tilting occur.

Today one can hike up Golden Canyon and literally walk through the last few million years of Death Valley geological history. Close to Furnace Creek, Golden Canyon is one of the most visited sites within Death Valley National Park. The turnoff into the canyon is just three miles south of the Visitor Center. Red clay, used by the Panamint Indians for body paint, can be clearly seen on the lower slopes of the hillsides near the canyon entrance.

DEATH VALLEY IN BLOOM

...these diversities offer endless possibilities for different types of growing things.

Roxanna Ferris,
Death Valley Wildflowers, 1981

Above: Desert Five Spot (Eremalche rotundifolium). *Top, right: Wildflowers add a carpet of color to the Joshua Tree forest near Lee Flat.*

Death Valley may have been described by weary pioneers as devoid of greenery, but in fact a remarkable diversity of plant life is found here. Over 1,000 plant species occur within the Park, a list that includes ten different species of ferns, six lilies, two orchids, and a unique species of palm. At least twenty-six flowering plant species that bloom here are found nowhere else in the world—including the delicate white-flowered Eureka Dunes evening primrose, the exuberant yellow Panamint daisy, and the blue-blossomed Death Valley sage.

Visitors may hope to see vast panoramas of spring wildflowers, but not every winter sees sufficient precipitation to make the desert bloom. Above-average rainfall must occur in November and December to germinate a profusion of seeds. Additional rain in January and February allows the flowering plants continued growth and the promise of maximum bloom. Then, with the first warm days of late February and early March, rapid development of the stems and buds occurs, followed shortly thereafter by the simultaneous appearance of millions of flowers. Within Death Valley National Park some of the best wildflowers displays are in the south end of the park, where desert gold poppies, sand verbena, lupine, and sunflowers grow close to the roadside for easy viewing and photographing.

Cacti, like wildflowers, can often be viewed during driving excursions through the Park. The Death Valley region has at least thirteen varieties of cacti including calico, old man, cottontop, and Mojave mound cactus. With the sole exception of the cottontop cactus, cacti bloom in the spring and all produce large and beautiful flowers. The showy magenta blossoms of the beavertail cactus, one of Death Valley's most abundant species, can be seen from many of the roads which traverse gravelly soils above 1,000-foot elevations. Beavertail cacti are particularly noticeable along the road north to Scottys Castle.

Two species of yucca occur within Death Valley National Park boundaries: the Mojave yucca and the Joshua tree.

Considered the symbol of the California desert, the Joshua tree can grow up to forty feet in height. Each individual tree displays a unique style of branching. Stands of Joshua trees can be seen along the road to the Racetrack and at Lee Flat.

Death Valley plants utilize three broad methods to cope with their arid habitat. The seeds of annual or "ephemeral" plants lie dormant throughout most of the year, germinating only after winter rains moisten the soil. They grow rapidly, develop flowers and seeds within a few short weeks, and then die as summer approaches. Creosote, cacti, and other perennials endure drought conditions by collecting water through specialized root systems. They conserve this moisture several ways—reducing leaf size, shedding leaves entirely, or closing down pores in the leaf surfaces during daylight hours. Other plants evade arid conditions by growing in places where runoff from storms collects. Arrow weed and salt bushes are most frequent on the valley floor where subsurface moisture collects. Cottonwoods and true willows are common at higher elevations near canyon springs.

Top, left: Desert mariposa (Calochortus kennedyi) *bursts into color on the slopes of the Nelson Range in Saline Valley. Center left: Stream Orchis,* (Epipactis gigantea), *a member of the orchid family, blooms in high, wet Surprise Canyon in the Panamint Mountains. Top, right: Calthaleaf phacelia* (Phacelia calthifolia) *and Desert sunflower* (Gerea canescens) *thrive on the valley floor near Golden Canyon. Left, above: Englemann's hedgehog cactus* (Enchinocereus engelmannii) *and Desert Indian paintbrush* (Castilleja chromosa) *peek from a rock crevice. Left: Desert sand verbena* (Abronia villosa) *and Shredding evening primrose* (Camassonia boothii condensata) *emerge from the sandy soil of valleys and alluvial fans.*

WILDROSE CHARCOAL KILNS

Ten perfectly-aligned stone charcoal kilns, well-preserved remains of Death Valley's early mining period, are located in upper Wildrose Canyon in the Panamint Mountains. Each kiln stands twenty-five feet high with an average diameter of approximately thirty-one feet. Chinese laborers constructed the Swiss-designed kilns in 1877. Native rocks, bound with mortar, were used as building stones. The beehive shape of the kilns was considered desirable for strength and efficiency in manufacturing charcoal, sorely needed to fire the smelters at the Modoc Mine in the Argus Mountains, just fifteen miles west of Wildrose Canyon. This mine produced both lead and silver ore from deposits discovered in 1875. Wildrose Canyon in the Panamint Mountains, where pinyon pines covered the mountainsides, was the closest, most accessible location where fuel was available

The Wildrose Charcoal Kilns, built in 1877 to produce charcoal to fire smelters for a nearby mine, stand in Wildrose Canyon with a wide vista west toward the Sierra Nevada Range.

for making charcoal. It is said that Panamint Indians were hired to cut the pinyon pine logs used in the kilns. It took a long work day to fill the kilns with pinyon logs and another fifteen days before the charcoal was ready to be transported the fifteen miles to the smelter at the Modoc Mine. The Wildrose Charcoal Kilns operated for only two or three years, from 1877 to perhaps 1880. Improved smelting procedures abroad resulted in ores being shipped elsewhere to be refined; the last smelter in the Death Valley region had probably shut down by 1885. The kilns have been restored twice and thus appear much as they did when in operation.

MOSAIC CANYON

One of the finest hikes in Death Valley can be found just southwest of Stove-

pipe Wells Village, at the end of an improved dirt road. Mosaic Canyon enters Tucki Mountain from the north and immediately penetrates the water-polished white, gray, and black eroded fragments of rock that comprise a "mosaic." These rocks have been re-cemented together after having been broken apart, transported, and then buried at their present location millions of years ago. Originally part of what geologists call the Noonday Dolomite formation, these rocks now form Mosaic Canyon's steep right-hand canyon wall. A large fault later split the beds apart, allowing the downcutting force of moving water to form a canyon along the fault. As one walks up the canyon, the mosaic floor is occasionally exposed through the coarse sand and gravel of the canyon bottom. Patches of pure white marble can also be seen on the canyon walls.

Above, left: The smooth, polished rock walls of Mosaic Canyon are inviting to hikers. Top: Details of eroded marble walls and polished "breccia"—rock composed of sharp fragments embedded in fine sand. Left: Mushroom Rock, an exposed basalt formation south of Furnace Creek.

21

SAND DUNES

Wind creates ever-shifting patterns in the surface of sand dunes. Desert creatures leave evidence of their passing among the ripples—beetles and a kangaroo rat traversed the dune, top. A sidewinder rattlesnake (Crotalus cerastes) *makes a distinctive s-shaped mark crossing the sand.*

The popular view of deserts is one of endless plains of sand piled into huge dunes. In fact, Death Valley National Park is typical of desert environments throughout the world: less than 5 percent is covered in dune sand. Though they constitute a minor part of the desert landscape, sand dunes have unique qualities. Compared with other harsh arid environments, the dunes have a softer, more gentle appearance. Dunes appear inviting, and—in the low light conditions of early morning and late afternoon—almost seem to be illuminated from within. Sand dunes are also dynamic. With every major windstorm individual grains are transported and redeposited, thus altering both the shape and position of the dunes. Finally, the ecological

requirements of many plant and animal species, such as the Eureka Evening Primrose and Mojave Fringe-toed Lizard, are only satisfied in dune habitats.

Of six dune systems in Death Valley National Park, the fifteen square miles of dunes near Stove Pipe Wells Village are the most conspicuous and certainly the most accessible. The sand here is a product of erosion from the Cottonwood Mountains to the west and northwest. A close examination of individual grains reveals both light and dark fragments: black grains are a combination of iron and oxygen known as magnetite; the white grains are quartz.

With their enormous height, scenic splendor, and unique plant species, the remote Eureka Dunes are the most scientifically-important dunes in Death Valley National Park. Tucked away in the southeast corner of Eureka Valley in the northern end of the Park, the Eureka Dunes reach nearly 700 feet from top to bottom, making them the tallest sand dunes in California. Their vertical relief is made all the more dramatic by the confined area of the dune complex; the entire system stretches just three and a half miles in length and one mile in width. On winter afternoons the dunes make for ideal landscape photography as they rise from the desert in front of the rugged Last Chance Mountains immediately to the east. The Eureka Dunes host over fifty distinct plant species, all of which are most noticeable in the spring following years of abundant winter rains. Three plant species found here—Eureka Dunegrass, Eureka Evening Primrose, and Eureka Milk-vetch are exceedingly rare and found nowhere else in the world. Other dune systems can be found in Saline Valley, at the north end of the Panamint Valley, and near the southern boundary of the park near Saratoga Springs.

An early morning or late afternoon visit to the dunes reveals one of the more intriguing aspects of their appearance—evenly spaced ripples. These ripples are tiny piles of heavy sand grains that accumulate at a perpendicular angle to the wind. Simply explained, winds of varying velocities sort out different sized grains with the larger grains lagging behind, forming long ridges.

Sand dunes have their own unique assemblage of plants and animals. Sand verbena, brown-eyed primrose, and certain varieties of locoweed are often associated with dune systems. The sidewinder rattlesnake, desert kangaroo rat, and kit fox appear to reach their greatest abundance in areas of loose, windblown sand. These animals can often be detected by walking out onto the dunes in the early morning and looking for their tracks—evidence of activity the night before.

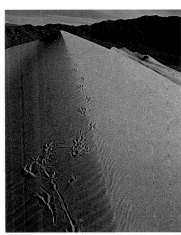

Top: The Eureka Sand Dunes, tallest sand dunes in California, stand in the remote valley west of the Last Chance Range in the far northern corner of the Park. Left: The Eureka evening primrose (Oenothera californica ssp. eurekensis), an endangered species found only in the Eureka Dunes. Below: Tracks ascend a steep dune for a birds-eye view of the Eureka Valley.

Death Valley National Park now protects six dune systems: in Death Valley at Mesquite Flats near Stovepipe Wells; in the far south of the Park near Saratoga Springs; at the north end of the Panamint Valley; in the center of the Saline Valley; and two separate dune areas in the northeast and northwest parts of the Eureka Valley.

*Above: The Panamint
Dunes and the north end
of the Panamint Valley.
Left: Eureka dunegrass,
an endemic and endangered
species now protected within
Death Valley National Park.
Opposite: Ripple patterns
cover the sand dunes at
Death Valley on a winter
afternoon, contrasting with
the rugged slopes of the
Grapevine Mountains to
the northwest.*

WILDLIFE IN DEATH VALLEY

...the first law of the desert to which animal life of every kind pays allegiance is the law of endurance and abstinence.

John C. Van Dyke,
The Desert, 1901

Above: A brown-headed cowbird (Molothrus ater) *rests on a blooming Joshua Tree. Top, right: A trio of desert bighorn sheep* (Ovis canadensis) *traverse a rocky habitat high in the desert mountains. The rams grow spectacular curved horns and may weigh over 200 pounds; ewes grow narrower horns and reach 75 to 130 pounds. Bighorn sheep have exceptional climbing skills and strong constitutions— easily crossing steep rugged terrain and feeding on dry, tough desert plants.*

The varied terrain and types of habitat in Death Valley National Park support a surprising variety of animal life. No less than 451 vertebrate animals are known to occur within park boundaries, including six kinds of amphibians, 37 reptile species, 347 species of birds, 58 different mammals, and four species of pupfish found nowhere else in the world.

Without question Death Valley's most picturesque animal is the bighorn sheep. A mature ram may reach 200 pounds and, with its muscular torso and massive curled horns, is the largest native animal within the Park boundaries. Bighorns are partial to rocky mountainsides; a glimpse of one is usually reserved for the more ambitious hiker. About five hundred bighorn sheep make their home in the mountains of Death Valley National Park.

The cat-sized kit fox is occasionally seen scampering across roadways at night. These large-eared canines become active at dusk as they begin searching for kangaroo rats and rabbits, their chief prey. Ringtails, bobcats, grey foxes, and mountain lions are among the larger predators within the Park, but like the bighorn sheep and kit foxes, these animals are rarely seen. The coyote is the carnivore most often observed by visitors, regularly spotted around Furnace Creek during the winter months.

The smaller animal inhabitants of Death Valley are those most frequently seen by park visitors. The antelope ground squirrel, distinguished by striped sides and a tail conspicuously white underneath, is common in areas of coarse soil and rock. Jet black ravens may be observed on most any day, usually as they glide overhead in search of food scraps at campgrounds or perhaps a jackrabbit carcass on the road. Roadrunners nest in the trees and shrubs surrounding Furnace Creek Ranch and other parts of the park where insects and the ubiquitous side-blotched lizard are common. The latter reptile is characterized by a two-inch body adorned with light stripes (female) or speckled with blue and yellow (male). Side-blotched lizards might be seen basking on rocks on any calm day, even in winter when all other reptiles are in hibernation.

Many visitors to Death Valley fear they must contend with venomous creatures such as rattlesnakes, scorpions, or centipedes, but in truth these animals are rarely encountered. The vast majority of visitors never see any of the species of rattlesnake that occur within park boundaries. Scorpions are nocturnal and thus active when visitors are in their tents, campers or hotel rooms—and none of the scorpion species within Death Valley are considered dangerous to humans. In fact, the most unusual creature that visitors might encounter is the large spider known as the tarantula. Males are often seen in the fall months, when they search for mates. Ferocious as they may appear, tarantulas are quite harmless.

In large part the diversity of animal life that exists within Death Valley National Park is a testament to the superb behavioral adaptations these animals have made to their environment. Unlike plants that have no choice but to endure environmental extremes, animals are mobile and can move into more favorable micro-environments when advantageous. Many

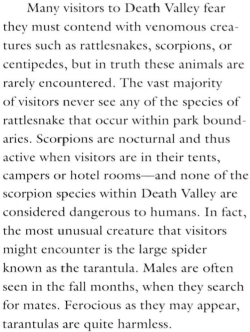

desert animals are nocturnal, becoming active at night when temperatures are lower and the air more humid. Small animals such as pocket mice, kangaroo rats, and ground squirrels—and even large animals, such as bobcats—burrow underground where temperatures may never rise above 80 degrees Fahrenheit. White-crowned sparrows, western blue-birds, and ruby-crowned kinglets spend only the mild winters in Death Valley. With the onset of warmer weather they fly away to milder climates.

Clockwise, from top left: A pair of mating roadrunners (Geococcyc californianus); *the male offers a small rodent as part of courtship. Desert coyotes* (Canis latrans) *are smaller than their mountain cousins, with shorter, paler fur as an adaptation to desert habitat. A desert tortoise* (Gopherus agassizii), *searches out tasty spring wildflowers. The large, harmless desert tarantula* (Aphonopelma chalcodes) *may be seen in the fall, when males search day and night for a mate. The desert iguana* (Disposaurus dorsalis) *thrives in a hot, arid environment where it feeds on plants and insects. Iguanas retreat to a burrow in evening and hibernate during the winter months.*

DEVILS CORNFIELD

Just southeast of Stovepipe Wells Village stands a curious arrangement of plants that from a distance resemble corn shocks. These plants are clumps of arrow weed, *Pluchea sericea*, a member of the sunflower family. Arrow weed is widely distributed in Death Valley, wherever groundwater rises close to the surface. Here wind erosion has removed the uppermost layers of soil except where the roots of the perennial have held it fast—a process called "deflation." Each clump reflects a point at which water is close enough to the surface to support the arrow weed.

SALT CREEK AND PUPFISH

Surprises also occur in this land of extremes: a perennial stream complete with fish exists in the center of Death Valley. Fifteen miles north of the Park Visitor Center lies Salt Creek—smack in the middle of the hottest, driest place

Top: At Salt Creek, spring-fed water runs year-round. Above: Distinctive cornstalk-like clumps of arrow weed at Devils Cornfield.

in North America. As its name implies, the water is salty, comparable to the salinity of ocean water. The salt deposits found along the edge of the stream contain carbonate and sulfate but are mostly sodium chloride or table salt. The water originates in the Mesquite Flat drainage basin, two miles north of historic Stovepipe Wells, but does not flow on the surface until it reaches McLean Springs. Salt Creek is a result of rock layers which have been up-lifted along faults, allowing ground water to reach the surface.

As one might expect, the water attracts a number of plants and animals that would not otherwise survive here. Certainly the most interesting Salt Creek denizen is one species of pupfish, *Cyprinodon salinus*, which is found no-where else in the world. This species is considered a relic from a time thousands of years ago when Death Valley was part of a huge river and lake system that began in the Sierra Nevada to the west and ended in Death Valley. Pupfish were more widely distributed at that time, but as the region became increasingly arid since the close of the Pleistocene Epoch ten thousand years ago, and the connecting rivers and lakes vanished, this species has become endemic to Death Valley. Now it is totally isolated and confined to Salt Creek.

Pupfish lie dormant in the mud at the bottom of the creek during winter and are rarely seen. By March they are active again, with males establishing underwater territories which they defend against intrusion by other males. Spawning has been known to occur as early as February and continues through summer in the deeper pools. Young pupfish reach maturity in two to three months, and several generations can be produced each year. Pupfish feed on algae, tiny insects, crustaceans, and snails which they may scoop from the bottom or, in moving water, capture while the food drifts by.

Pupfish are among the most heat-tolerant fish. They can stand temperatures

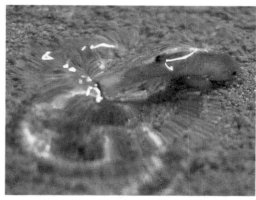

from 104 to 111 degrees Fahrenheit as well as daily fluctuations in water temperature spanning 36 degrees. Some pupfish are also strikingly tolerant of high salinity levels, and can survive in water up to 3.7 times saltier than seawater.

Surface water attracts many other animals to the vicinity of Salt Creek. Great blue herons, common snipes, spotted sandpipers, and killdeers have all been seen along or in Salt Creek. Herons are known to capture and consume pupfish. Coyotes and kit foxes have also been seen in the area. In earlier times Panamint Indians fished for pupfish, using large porous baskets to scoop them up. Piles of fish were then baked between layers of tule reeds and hot ashes.

Above: A lush oasis at Darwin Falls, west of the Panamint Valley in the Argus Mountains. Left: Pupfish live in the hot, salty waters of Salt Creek.

29

Top: The shallow, salty lake
at Saline Valley's lowest
point reflects the rugged
Saline Range to the east.
Pure salt was mined here
in the early 1900s.
Above: Wetlands at
Saratoga Springs, in the
Park's far southern region.
Right: A waterfall tumbles
out of Surprise Canyon, in
the Panamint Range.

ROCK ART

Engravings and paintings preserved on rock surfaces are evidence of a time thousands of years ago and a people who lived and hunted in the Death Valley region. Engravings or "petroglyphs" — designs chipped or scored into the faces of rocks—are much more abundant in Death Valley National Park than paintings or "pictographs." In Greenwater Canyon both forms of rock art can be found. Although much of the artwork consists of unfamiliar patterns and designs, numerous forms can be recognized including lizards, snakes, scorpions, deer, bighorn sheep, and dancing humans. Excellent examples of rock art can be seen in Death Valley National Park at Echo Canyon, Cottonwood Canyon, and Klare Spring in Titus Canyon. At many of these sites it is obvious that certain designs are older than others. Sometimes one figure may be drawn over another, or one design may

be lighter in color and seem "fresher" than another. Because petroglyphs were scratched into the surface of the rock, the dark surface stains of iron and manganese oxides were removed, revealing the untainted rock beneath. "Desert varnish" stains on rock surfaces accumulate with time and thus petroglyphs darken as they become older. Some of the rock art here is thought to be thousands of years old, made by people of the so-called Mesquite Flat Culture who lived within Death Valley from approximately 3,000 B.C. until 1 A.D.

Above: Granite tors punctuate a rocky hillside northeast of Hunter Mountain. Left: Petroglyphs etched into the dark surfaces of a rock depict bighorn sheep. Rock art is evidence of the presence of long-ago humans—ancestors of Native Americans—who left these messages on rock. Obviously they had sufficient time to be creative and to communicate non-verbally with others, although we cannot know the exact meaning of the designs.

UBEHEBE CRATER

Some 4,000 years ago, a tremendous explosion occurred in Death Valley, undoubtedly heard and felt by the native people inhabiting the area at the time. Not far from the present day location of Scottys Castle, a rising plume of molten basalt came in contact with the overlying watertable. The water instantaneously flashed to steam, creating an explosive pressure that knocked off the mantle of sedimentary rock above and blew a crater in the ground one-half mile across and 500 feet deep. The crater would become known in Panamint Indian legends as "the basket in the ground." Today this site of volcanic activity is called Ubehebe Crater. There are actually several explosion craters in the area; Ubehebe is the largest and most recently created. Volcanic cinders and ash, in some places 150 feet thick, cover the ground from two to five miles in every direction.

Top: Ubehebe Crater was created when a huge plume of lava came in contact with the underground water table; the water turned to steam and blew a huge hole in the ground. Above: An aerial view of Ubehebe and Little Hebe craters, at the north end of the Cottonwood Mountains.

THE RACETRACK

One of the most intriguing places within Death Valley National Park is a dry lake called the "Racetrack." Large boulders, some weighing as much as four hundred pounds, have mysteriously moved across the dry lakebed, leaving gouged trails in the mud as evidence of their travels. No one has actually seen the rocks move, but scientists speculate that very strong winds blow the rocks across the lakebed when the mud surface is occasionally made slick by light rains and freezing temperatures.

Top: Trails left in the Racetrack's mud playa by "moving" boulders show curves, sharp angles, and intersections indicating the progress of each rock from year to year. Right: Boulders tumble down the steep hillside south of the Racetrack to rest on the dry lakebed below.

DEATH VALLEY HISTORY

...as we looked it seemed the most
God-forsaken country in the world.

William Manly, from *Death Valley in '49*, 1894.

The first humans who entered Death Valley 9,000 years ago encountered an environment quite different than the Death Valley of today. These people, ancestors of the historical Panamint Shoshone, found a place much friendlier—a land of cooler summers, greater rainfall, and an enormous lake that cov-ered the valley floor. The first people hunted large game animals like mastodons, giant ground sloths, and bison that fed on the abundant vegetation along the lake shore. Some time after the arrival of the first humans, for reasons of which we are still unsure, the climate here became warmer and drier as a result of the migration of most Pacific storm systems to higher latitudes. The result was the formation of desert conditions in Death Valley, and the harsh environment encountered by the first white people who entered there in 1849.

William Manly, John Rogers, and the "Jayhawker" party did not fully comprehend the challenge of the Mojave Desert when they headed out west. Perhaps their judgment was clouded by their quest for wealth. Gold had been discovered in California—and lay waiting for those hardy individuals who reached the goldfields first. The Jayhawkers, like thousands of other easterners to follow them, were unaccustomed to traveling through desert lands. None were prepared for a journey into the "valley of death."

On October 1, 1849, the Jayhawkers—along with several other parties heading for the California gold-fields—left the final staging point at Salt Lake City. Historical records indicate that this original amalgamation of westward travelers totaled 107 wagons with nearly two hundred eager gold-seekers aboard. A few days out of Salt Lake City, the emigrants encountered Captain Wesley Smith leading a pack-train of merchants to California. After much coaxing, Smith reluctantly shared with the Jayhawkers a map showing a route off the Old Spanish Trail that would lead them due west to Walker Pass. Such a shortcut would save weeks on the journey and take the Jayhawkers to the goldfields that much sooner. Eighty of the wagon drivers, however, played it safe and decided not to follow Smith's map. This group headed south toward San Bernardino in southern California. The remaining twenty-seven wagons followed Smith's map and headed due west toward Death Valley and some of the most rugged terrain in North America.

The group encountered extreme hardships. The twenty-seven wagons managed just fifteen arduous miles a day. The land offered little food; many of the oxen used to haul the wagons had to be slaughtered for meat. One by one, wagons were left behind and precious belongings sacrificed to the elements. Springs were few; more than once a mother would try to comfort her child who cried out for water. Splinter groups broke off from the original

Opposite: The rugged salt pan of Death Valley's floor.
Above: Weathered wood of a wagon at Harmony Borax Works.
Top: Sunrise on Telescope Peak, in the Panamint Range.

Viewed from the rocky Chloride Cliffs in the Funeral Mountains, Death Valley stretches south between the Amargosa and Panamint Ranges.

group devised a final desperate plan. The two youngest and most able-bodied men, Manly and John Rogers, agreed to leave the group at Bennett's Well and venture forth on foot over the mountains to seek food and assistance. The party felt sure that the village of Los Angeles must be just beyond the Panamints and that Manly and Rogers could return in not more than ten days with supplies. No one in the group could have known that Los Angeles was over two hundred miles away—Manly and Rogers would not make it back to Death Valley for over three weeks.

At first Manly and Rogers were no more successful on foot than with the wagons. They failed in their initial attempt to penetrate the mountain wall to the west but in their second attempt found a more southerly route through the Panamints and out of Death Valley. Heading south toward Los Angeles, they passed the corpse of a Mr. Fish, one of the bachelors they had parted with days before. He had died of exhaustion after escaping the valley. Even the gruesome site of Mr. Fish's swollen corpse did not deter Manly and Rogers from their rescue mission. After enduring nearly two weeks of thirst and hunger they succeeded in reaching Newhall, north of present-day Los Angeles, in early January. Spanish-speaking ranchers graciously provided them with food and pack animals for their return trip to Death Valley where their comrades were, hopefully, still alive and waiting.

Over twenty-one days had passed since Manly and Rogers had gone for help. They feared what they might find upon their return. On entering the valley they were distressed to discover the rotting corpse of Captain Culverwell, a member of their party. Was this the fate of everyone? Hours later, they spotted the lone wagon at Bennett's Well, but no sign of life. Nervously, Manly shot his rifle into the air. As if by magic a man got up from beneath the wagon and upon seeing Manly and Rogers shouted, "The boys have come, the boys have come!" Only the Bennett and Arcane families were left.

twenty-seven and sought their own way. In this condition the remnants of the Jayhawker party entered a long, narrow desert valley on Christmas Day, 1849.

Just before descending into the valley, a group of bachelors decided they must head north and broke ranks, leaving several weary families led by William Lewis Manly to continue west. Manly led his group—the Bennett family and several others—to a spring near Furnace Creek, where they could rest and await his return from a scouting mission in search of a passage out of the valley. In his absence, Indians killed three oxen in retribution for the group's theft of squashes several days earlier. To further add to their misery, Manly announced upon his return that no western or northern route existed through the rugged Panamint Mountains. If they were to have a chance of escaping the valley, they could only head south. One more long day's travel on foot led them to a source of water later to be named "Bennett's Well."

With only one wagon, almost no food, and faint from exhaustion, the

The others, such as Captain Culverwell, had struck out on their own when they feared that Manly and Rogers would never return. The fate of some of these individuals remains unknown to this day. Legend tells that one of the women, weakened and dreading the prospect of a hundred-mile march across the desert to Los Angeles, named the place of their suffering as they ascended the last ridge out of the valley. She looked back one last time, saying, "Goodbye, Death Valley."

At least three members of this Forty-Niners group perished crossing the desert, although only Captain Culverwell actually died within Death Valley proper. Tragically, he would not be the last of its victims. The valley's name would stick as tales of its horrors became immortalized—though often grossly exaggerated—by the press. The harsh desert, however, would continue to take its toll on miners, prospectors, and travelers.

MINERS AND FORTY-NINERS

Perhaps no region in the West is as closely linked with the burro-toting desert prospector than Death Valley. Prospectors by the thousands came; most left but a few stayed long enough to be buried in the land that never gave them the permanent wealth they sought. Shorty Harris, Cap Lemoigne, Seldom Seen Slim—all died penniless. Yet they spent their lives scouring the valley floor and surrounding mountains on the chance that they might strike it rich.

The tradition of mining and prospecting in the Death Valley region began with

the ill-fated Jayhawker Party and their stories of the Lost Gunsight Mine. While struggling out of the valley in 1849, one of the Jayhawkers, an unknown Mississippian, by chance picked up a piece of silver ore while looking for the gunsight which had fallen off his rifle. It is believed the ore came from a rock outcrop along Emigrant Wash, somewhere between the present-day Stovepipe Wells Village and Emigrant Ranger Station. That night, around the campfire, the Mississippian whittled a new gunsight from the silver in the rock. Short of food and water, neither he nor any of the Jayhawkers could afford to linger at the place of discovery and were forced to proceed towards Los Angeles. By the time they reached civilization, six weeks later, talk of the small silver fragment had mushroomed into tales of "a mountain of silver" and Death Valley's first mining boom was born.

Hundreds of prospectors came in search of the Lost Gunsight Mine, including William Manly and Asahel Bennett of 49er fame. These two men returned to Death Valley in 1862 but failed to locate the silver ore outcrop. In 1864 a party led by Darwin French also failed to locate the Gunsight but did find the old Antimony Mine above present-day Wildrose Ranger

Death Valley's colorful mining past is still evident in the remnants of old mining operations. Above, left: The entrance to a long-abandoned mine. Above: The Lost Burro Mine, high in the Cottonwood Mountains.

Above: A weathered shack and ore cart tracks at the Inyo Mine, Echo Canyon. Maroni Hicks and Chet Leavitt discovered gold here in 1905. Right: Oil boilers at Harmony Borax Works.

Station. This latter mine, discovered a few years earlier, was probably the first to operate in Death Valley. To this day the fate of the Lost Gunsight Mine remains a mystery.

Panamint City was the first real boom town to spring up in the Death Valley region. Located not in the desert, but high in the Panamint Mountains, its beginnings were unusual to say the least. In the winter of 1873, five bandits robbed a Wells Fargo stage and made off with an express box filled with silver bullion. They fled into the Panamint Mountains via Surprise Canyon. Well-stocked with provisions, they counted on their remote location and strategic position to ward off any law officers that might come searching for them. They planned to wait a few months until interest in their evil deed cooled down.

During their exile in the Panamints, one of the bandits discovered a vein of silver ore—one so big that it made their stolen box of bullion seem pitifully insignificant. Not surprisingly, they were reluctant to leave their fortress and go into the nearest town to file a claim. Their only

recourse was to try and square things with the Wells Fargo Company, but that would take some delicate negotiating. Luckily, one of the desperados knew Senator William M. Stewart of nearby Nevada, a tough politician known throughout the West as a great promoter of silver mining. One of the robbers was able to sneak away from the hideout and ask the Senator to act as a go-between with the Wells Fargo Company. Although the precise details vary from one account to the next, it seems that Senator Stewart, after eyeing the ore samples supplied by the bandit, got Wells Fargo to agree to a repayment settlement. In return, the Senator received a very large share in the mining interest of the robbers. With all parties in agreement, the robbers filed their claims and Panamint silver became the talk of the West. The rush to the Panamint Mountains was on.

In less than one year a city appeared—complete with a newspaper, saloons, and an abundance of dance-hall girls. Although the thousand or so inhabitants would not make Panamint City the big-

Left: The twenty-mule team
wagons, on display at
Harmony Borax Works.
Each huge wagon—the rear
wheels stand seven feet
high—could carry a ten-ton
payload of crytallized borax.
Teams of twenty mules drew
the wagons over 165 miles of
rough desert terrain to the
nearest railhead at Mojave.
Above: A mule-driver and
his swamper, circa 1886.

gest boom town ever to appear in the Death Valley region, the fortune-hunters it attracted certainly made it the toughest.

Fearful that members of the town's criminal element might conspire to rob wagon shipments of silver headed toward the railhead, one mine owner devised a plan that would thwart the boldest high-wayman. Senator Stewart directed his mill boss to cast the silver into 700-pound cannon balls, to be loaded into freight wagons and shipped without guards. There was only one road out of the Panamints and no place for bandits to divert a cargo of such size. And robbers did not have the necessary means to melt down the huge silver balls into something more manageable. Not surprisingly, no holdups ever took place and the shipments arrived safely at their destination.

By the late 1870s Panamint City's silver ore had become difficult to extract and mining enthusiasm began to wane. When successive floods wiped out the town's buildings and access road, most people packed up and headed for more fertile pickings. By the 1880s one of

Death Valley's greatest boom towns had become one of its best known ghost towns.

THE TWENTY MULE TEAMS

The story of borax and the twenty-mule teams in Death Valley began in 1873 when the Inyo Independent newspaper announced that the mineral had been discovered on the valley floor. Nonetheless, the initial claims were not developed until eight years later, in 1881, when Aaron Winters of nearby Ash Meadows, Nevada, sold his Death Valley claim for $20,000 to William T. Coleman of San Francisco. Coleman was an entrepreneur already involved in borax mining in Nevada. The strike, one mile north of Furnace Creek, became known as the Harmony Borax Works. Here Coleman's Greenland Salt and Borax Company erected several adobe and stone buildings, wooden warehouses, a boiler, and thirty-six huge crystallization tanks.

The valuable "white stuff" was not immediately ready for industrial use. At the Harmony claim, borax appeared as soft white fluff around the marsh on the valley

Top: A prospector loading his mule with supplies. Above: Newspapers and broadsides encouraged miners and opportunists to come to Greenwater. A copper mining boom began here in 1906 but just a year later Greenwater was a ghost town. Right: On display at the Borax Museum at Furnace Creek Ranch, this water-powered gold arrastra was used in the 1880s to grind ore .

floor. The fluff was collected by Chinese laborers, placed in large baskets, and hauled to the Harmony refinery on sledges. At the refinery, borax was allowed to crystallize on iron rods suspended in large vats. Things went well during the winter of 1883–1884, but the refining process failed during the summer months when high temperatures prevented the borax from crystallizing. Coleman's company overcame the problem by moving the operation close to the town of Shoshone, near another source of borax, during the summer months. Although less than fifty miles from Furnace Creek, Shoshone had cooler summer temperatures due to its higher elevation. The last and most serious obstacle to the commercial success of Coleman's operation was getting the refined borax to market over miles of rocky, rugged desert.

Coleman's solution involved the use of durable mules—several teams of them—to pull giant wagons through the desert. The enormous hauling wagons were constructed solely for the Death Valley borax shipments. Probably the largest wagons ever used, each could carry a ten-ton payload. The rear wheels stood seven feet high and were protected with steel tires eight inches wide and an inch thick. The wagon beds stretched sixteen

feet and were four feet wide with sides six feet high. Empty, each wagon weighed 7,800 pounds. It is not clear who designed them but historian L. Burr Belden believes that at least some of the wagons were built in San Bernardino by the Bright and Chute Wagon Works for a cost of about $900 apiece. Considering the difficulty of the terrain over which they traveled, the wagons were remarkably free of breakdowns during the five years they were in use. Only the steel tires had to be replaced with any regularity.

One hundred sixty-five miles of treacherous desert separated Death Valley from the railhead at Mojave. Waterholes were fifty miles apart with dusty, rocky, sandy ruts serving for roads in between. The twenty-mule teams traveled from fifteen to seventeen miles a day, resulting in a journey of ten days between the Harmony Borax Works and the railhead. Two men rode the wagons: the driver and his assistant, called a "swamper." Generally speaking the teamsters were men of few words, were without wives or children, and were considered reliable employees who could be trusted with the $10,000 to $15,000 worth of property under their supervision. Journalist John Spears, writing in 1892, described the mule-driver's occupation:

> *The life of a teamster on the desert is not only one of hardship, it is in places extremely dangerous. There are grades, like the one on the road from Granite Spring to Mojave, where the plunge is steep, the roadbed as hard as a turnpike. The load must go down, so when the brink is reached, the driver throws his weight on the brake in the front wagon, the swamper handles the brake on the rear, and away they go, creaking, groaning and gliding, until the bottom is reached.*

For five years, from 1883 to 1888, the twenty-mule teams delivered their loads to Mojave with surprising precision, considering the difficulty of the terrain and the scorching summertime temperatures. It was a reasonably profitable venture for Coleman and no doubt would have remained that way were it not for Coleman's poor investments in other enterprises, the discovery of borax deposits closer to rail lines, and the development of new processing technology. Much later, the romance and adventure spurred by the long haul of the twenty-mule teams from Death Valley would become an advertising symbol for the U.S. Borax Company and the popular radio and television show "Death Valley Days" which it sponsored.

THE BOOM TOWN OF GREENWATER

"Here today and gone tomorrow" best describes Greenwater. In 1906 the town's population totalled seventy. Then in just one month it jumped to 1,000 with over 2,500 mining claims staked out in the surrounding hills. Greenwater would be promoted as "The Greatest Copper Camp on Earth," yet by December 1907—just thirteen months later—the town was abandoned. The stampede began in 1906 as a result of a prospector's discovery and filing for a mining claim along the eastern slopes of the Black Mountains. The mineral was not gold, silver or even borax, but a greenish ore containing copper. Rumors were rampant about the extent of the deposits. Some enthusiasts claimed the ground was 75 percent copper for seventy square miles!

The news traveled like wildfire and investors popped up everywhere. There seemed no shortage of capital, with as much as $200,000 being paid for those claims that were staked first. Stock was made available in New York with shares going for up to $250 each. Arthur Kunze, the prospector who filed the first claim, received $150,000 for his mineral rights, much of it in the form of stock in a syndicate that would become known as the Greenwater Copper Mine and Smelter Company.

But there was just one problem with mining copper in the Greenwater district—there was very little copper. As the miners discovered after only a few months, the veins went "neither down, up, nor sideways." When the news got out that Greenwater copper simply was not materializing as hoped, money vanished overnight, stock became worthless, and almost every newspaper office, bank, boarding house, and store was vacated within thirty days. In short, Greenwater became one of the best examples of the get-rich-quick schemes so prevalent among eastern businessmen who looked to the West for their new fortunes.

GOLD IN DEATH VALLEY

In only two locations within the Death Valley region was gold mining ever profitable: around the town of Skidoo and at the Keane Wonder Mine. The mines surrounding Skidoo held the relatively unusual distinction of having made money for their owners. Between 1905 and 1917 nearly six million dollars in gold was extracted at a cost of about

Weathered towers and rusted equipment are all that remain of the early twentieth-century gold mining operation at the Keane Wonder Mine, high in the Funeral Mountains near the Nevada border.

The evaporation ponds at Saline Valley. Between 1913 and 1920 an aerial tramway connected the salt mining operation here to the Owens Valley, on the west side of the rugged Inyo Mountains.

three million. Such profits explained why both telephone and stage service existed at Skidoo, luxuries few other boom towns possessed. What Skidoo didn't have when it was founded was water. No spring existed near the mines, so water had to be piped in from Telescope Peak, twenty-three miles away. Born from this project was the then-popular slang expression "twenty-three skidoo," a popular way of saying "scram" or get lost.

Skidoo was peaceful by mining town standards. Yet it became famous for a sensational murder, or rather the peculiar publicity surrounding the murder. It seems a drunken saloon keeper named Joe "Hooch" Simpson shot the town banker dead. The law-abiding citizens promptly hanged Simpson and buried him. Unfortunately, it took several days for a Herald reporter covering the story to arrive from Los Angeles; he missed the hanging by just twenty-four hours. His story—perhaps fabricated—says the townsfolk, honored by the presence of a big city reporter and eager not to disappoint him, promptly dug up Simpson and hanged him again. The reporter got his photographs and the seven hundred residents of Skidoo had their town name in print across the country.

Another profitable gold-mining operation was the Keane Wonder Mine, located in the Funeral Mountains on the east side of Death Valley. In 1903 Jack Keane and Domingo Atcheson discovered gold ore that was so impressive that they sold their claim for $150,000 even before any digging began. The investment paid off and by 1907 a twenty-stamp mill was in operation crushing 1,800 tons of ore each month. The mill's unique tramway system was constructed to use the weight of the descending ore to generate power for the crushers. Today, a high clearance road leads visitors to the old mill foundation, tram towers, and a rusting bullwheel—all that remain of the operation. A one-mile trail leads up the mountainside to the mine.

THE SALT TRAM

To the west and north of Death Valley lies Saline Valley. As its name suggests, salt deposits cover the valley floor—salt so pure that no refinement is necessary before use. In the early 1900s the salt was easily harvested but transporting the salt out of the valley was difficult and uneconomical. White Smith, a former teamster with the Death Valley borax operation and a mineral claim holder in Saline Valley, conceived of a possible solution. An aerial tramway could be built that ran from the floor of the Saline Valley at approximately 1,100 feet, to the crest of the Inyo Mountains at 8,720 feet and down to the railhead at Swansea in the Owens Valley to the west. The total distance would be about thirteen miles; the cost of such a tram was estimated at $500,000.

With financing secured, construction was begun in 1911 and continued for two years until 1913. When completed, it was—and still is today—the longest aerial tramway ever built. Unfortunately, the tram's design was faulty. Breakdowns were common and the heavily laden salt buckets were simply too heavy for the tram design to handle. By 1920 the tram

had ceased to operate. Visitors to Saline Valley today can still see the wooden tram towers leading up into the rugged Inyo Mountains.

DEATH VALLEY SCOTTY

Death Valley Scotty was unquestionably the region's most famous prospector—yet he probably never made a nickel from a mine or vein of precious metal. For decades he was thought to be the wealthiest man ever to strike it rich in the Death Valley region and, in one respect, he had done just that.

The youngest of six children, Death Valley Scotty (his real name was Walter E. Scott) was born in Kentucky on September 20, 1872. His father bred and trained trotting horses and Scotty was raised to be comfortable and confident in the saddle. While still a boy, he traveled out West to join two of his older brothers and take on the life of a cowhand. The brothers ended up not far from Death Valley, at Humboldt Wells, Nevada. According to Scotty, he was not yet

fifteen when he got a job as a swamper on one of the famed twenty-mule team wagons out of the Harmony Borax Works. Just how long he stayed with the Coleman Company is not known but in 1890 he was "discovered" by a talent scout from Buffalo Bill's Wild West Show. He accepted a job as a roper, shooter and trick rider.

Scotty traveled throughout the United States and Europe for the next eleven years as part of Buffalo Bill's show. He loved the spotlight, and although he never became one of the show's headliners, his experience at this point in his career influenced the rest of his life. He would never be content as a spectator. A disagreement with Buffalo Bill finally led Scotty to leave the Wild West Show. Although Scotty's career as a trick rider was over, another more profitable career was about to begin.

Through contacts he had made while with the Wild West Show he was able to arrange a meeting with Julian Gerard, a wealthy businessman from New York.

Left: A portrait of young Walter Scott at his writing desk. Top: Albert Johnson and his friend Scotty at Death Valley Ranch. Above: Bessie and Albert Johnson.

An overview of Scottys Castle, nestled in a canyon in the Grapevine Mountains at the northern end of Death Valley, with Tin Mountain to the west.

Scotty carried two gold nuggets when he arrived at Gerard's office in 1902. He convinced Gerard that they were from a gold mine Scotty had discovered: If Gerard would grubstake him, the gold mine could be reopened and mined, bringing in a fortune for both of them. Gerard was no fool, but one must consider the climate of the times. To an Easterner, the West was a land of exploration and excitement. Scotty offered a piece of this excitement—and the possibility of a tremendous return for a relatively small investment.

Gerard's $10,000 enabled Scotty to assemble the best pack outfits money could buy. But he did not spend much time digging for gold. According to a Daggett storekeeper "he spent far more time in the saloons than he did on the desert." Los Angeles newspaper accounts from that time tell of a "W. Scott of

Death Valley who paid for everything with hundred dollar bills and was renowned for his generous tipping of bellboys and chambermaids while staying at the best hotels the city had to offer." When Scotty returned to New York and told Gerard that he was not able to relocate the mine which had held so much promise, Gerard was left with "nothing to show for it but a pile of correspondence and two gold nuggets."

When Gerard refused to provide additional grubstake funds, Scotty was left without a sponsor. But not for long. In 1904, Scotty met Albert M. Johnson, an insurance executive from Chicago. Johnson and Scotty were opposites in almost every way. Scotty was gregarious and loud; Johnson was shy and retiring. Scotty was a man of wafting morals often prone to activities that caused him trouble with the law; Johnson was deeply religious

Details of the interior of Scottys Castle, from left: The kitchen features colorful painted tile and hammered copper pans. The dining room displays Italian ceramic table settings, complete with the crest of Death Valley Ranch and the initials of Johnson and Scott. The iron and redwood courtyard gate also features Johnson and Scott's monogram.

and a respectable citizen in every way. But the most important difference between the two men was that Scotty, regardless of his claims to the contrary, was usually broke and in debt; Johnson was a millionaire with vast holdings in a number of successful enterprises. Strangely, the two would become lifelong companions and Johnson would become the only gold mine Scotty would ever know.

Acquaintances believed that Albert Johnson lived out his boyhood fantasies through Walter E. Scott; that Scotty was Johnson's entertainment. Whatever the reason for their friendship, it endured for over forty years. In October 1904, Scotty struck a deal with Johnson and his partner, Edward A. Shedd. The latter two men would receive two thirds of any mining properties or claims and Scotty would get what was left over. In turn Scotty would be grubstaked to the tune of $2,500 and would proceed immediately to the Death Valley region to get his mine operational. But Scotty had other ideas. After stopping briefly in Goldfield, Nevada, he headed, once again, to Los Angeles and embarked on a wild spending spree that got Scotty much publicity and resulted in Edward Shedd giving up any hopes of a return on his money. But Johnson's interest in Scotty's gold mine remained; in 1905 he

became a partner in Scotty's prospecting ventures.

With Johnson's financial backing Scotty's fortunes were certainly on the upswing and culminated in his most famous exploit: a record-breaking train ride. Quietly backed by the Santa Fe Railroad and Los Angeles businessman E. Burdon Gaylord, Scotty announced that he had hired his own special train to cover the distance between Los Angeles and Chicago faster than anyone before. The news media of the day gobbled up the story. Before the train departed on July 9, 1905, Scotty's exploit made newspaper headlines from coast to coast. On July 11 the train arrived in Chicago, having covered the 2,265-mile route in just under forty-five hours. The record was broken, the public was pleased, and Scotty was a national hero whose name was on the lips of millions of Americans.

In the early 1900s Albert Johnson made numerous trips into the Death Valley region with Scotty acting as guide and trail boss, a job no one could do as well as Walter E. Scott. Scotty was an excellent horseman and knew the Death Valley area as well as anyone. With his campfire stories of mines and prospectors it is hard to imagine anyone being better entertainment than Scotty.

45

Above: Details of the hand-forged ironwork on a gate at Scottys Castle. Center: The clock tower, complete with chimes, is decorated with colorful tile. Right: Moorish details on the castle exterior include a painted ceramic tile sundial, stucco walls, iron fixtures, and red roof tiles. Opposite: An arched stairway door frames a view of the entrance to Scottys Castle. The tower's weather vane features a prospector with his burro.

Though Scotty's gold mine was never found, Johnson became increasingly attached to the desert environment. By 1915 he had decided to spend a portion of each winter in Death Valley. His wife said she would accompany him on the condition that a proper home be constructed, suitable for entertaining the friends and relatives who might visit. Scotty would help find the site. Johnson began buying up land around Death Valley's northern boundaries with an eye on building a permanent residence. Construction on Johnson's "Death Valley Ranch" began in 1922. Although the house was not planned to be a castle, it had reached that stature by 1931 when the Great Depression brought all work to a halt.

The erection of such a building in Death Valley caused quite a stir amongst members of the press and throughout the construction period Scotty was highly visible. He even referred to the building as "my castle." All the while Johnson stayed in the background and seemed quite pleased not to have reporters clamoring at his heels. Eventually newspaper headlines dubbed the building "Scottys Castle," and Johnson seemed quite content to leave it that way.

The Moorish-style house is an impressive structure, especially considering its remote location. In the early construction phase, money was no object for multimillionaire Johnson. The castle interior was adorned with imported and hand-carved furniture; European artwork hung on every wall. A custom-made organ was moved into the music room, and the castle was outfitted with solar water heating and its own diesel generator to provide electricity. When work stopped in 1931, the castle contained over 31,000 square feet of floor space with stables, guest houses, and a 56-foot chimes tower. The Depression was rough on Johnson's finances and he could no longer afford to complete the castle's huge swimming pool (it still stands empty today) or finish the terraced landscaping that had originally been planned. Rather than attempt to rebuild his empire, he elected to retire and move out West. His last two residences were a home in the Hollywood Hills near Los Angeles, and of course his "castle" in Death Valley.

Throughout their retirement years Johnson and Scotty remained friends. Scotty always managed to keep busy entertaining the hundreds of people that came each winter to visit the castle. In 1948 Albert Johnson died, leaving the castle and ranch that surrounded it not to Scotty but to the Gospel Foundation of California, which Johnson had established. The Foundation did, however, allow Scotty to live on the premises and entertain the guests for the rest of his life. Scotty died in 1954 at the age of 82 and was buried on Windy Point, a hill overlooking his beloved castle.

Above: A rare, endemic Panamint Daisy (Enceliopsis covillei) *in Wildrose Canyon displays spectacular blooms—up to six inches across.*

Right: A view of Badwater, 282 feet below sea level in Death Valley, from lofty Aguereberry Point at 6,433 feet in the Panamint Range, demonstrates Death Valley's dramatic elevation changes.

Opposite: Brittlebush blooms in Galena Canyon, with a view north toward the snow-capped Panamint Range.

VISITING DEATH VALLEY TODAY

Death Valley is now a national park—in fact, the largest national park in the contiguous United States. The Desert Protection Act, passed by Congress on October 8 and signed into law by President William Clinton on October 31, 1994, forever changed the name of Death Valley National Monument to Death Valley National Park.

Far more important than the name change were changes in the park boundaries. The park's new configuration gave added protection to threatened and endangered species, including populations of desert tortoise in the remote Owlshead Mountains at the park's far southern boundary as well as the Eureka Evening Primrose in its far northern quarter. In addition, the Act added to the park seven new ecological systems, three noted mountain peaks, and three magnificent valleys for a total of 1.2 million additional acres. Today's Death Valley National Park encompasses 3,336,000 acres—its total area 57% larger than the old Death Valley National Monument.

With the increased size of an already large park, traveling through Death Valley has become a journey in itself. Give yourself ample time to visit the sites that are your first priority, and expect to return to Death Valley several times to see the Park's distant corners. Many popular visitor destinations in Death Valley—Scottys Castle, Zabriskie Point, and Dantes View—can be driven to on paved, regularly-patrolled roads. But be aware that some of the park's attractions—the Racetrack, the Joshua tree forest at Lee Flat, the historic Salt Tramway towers in Saline Valley, and the Eureka Sand Dunes—are accessible only on sparsely-traveled unpaved roads located in remote areas. Careful planning and high-clearance vehicles are important components of such trips. Enjoy Death Valley!